Zendipity Mindfulness

Carnival & Animals Adult COLORING Book

Stress & Anxiety Relief

Bold Patterns, & Large Print, Positive Affirmations

All aboard the Carnival Jamboree For a Colorful Expedition

Color Your World Calm

"My mindset is a powerful tool for change."

"Every day is a fresh start for me."

“I am worthy of success and love.”

"I choose to be happy & content."

"Great things happen when I think positively."

"My daily routine is filled with good things."

"My unique perspective leads me in the right direction."

"My daily routine is filled with good things."

"I am wonderfully fulfilled."

"I control my thoughts; they don't control me."

"I overcome challenges and expand my comfort zone."

"I am in control of my thoughts and emotions."

"I attract positive energy and positive people daily."

"I practice kindness and self-love everyday."

"My positive attitude shapes my daily life."

"I find good news and joy in everyday situations."

"I am in control of my thoughts and emotions."

"I make a significant difference in my life daily."

"I am the master of my thoughts and beliefs."

"I am in control of my destiny through positive thinking."

"I am worthy of success, love, and all good things."

"I am in charge of my life and my destiny."

"I turn difficult situations into personal growth."

"My journey of personal growth is a testament to my worth."

"My unique perspective leads me in the right direction."

"My thoughts shape my reality."

"I embrace positivity."

"I am resilient and capable of overcoming any challenge."

"I release all negative thoughts, banishing them from my mind."

"I am continually cultivating a life that is filled with joy, love, and abundance."

"Every day is an opportunity to release negativity and embrace the positivity that surrounds me."

"I shape my reality through the conscious choice to think positively."

"I welcome challenges as opportunities to expand my comfort zone."

"I Choose to see the good in every situation."

"I choose to be thankful in all things."

"I choose to be happy."

"I am worthy of love & respect."

"Everyday is a new beginning for success."

"I am more than my thoughts."

"I am more than enough."

"I am grateful for all that I have."

"I am fulfilled."

“Today I choose to smile.”

"This is an awesome day."

"I have more than enough."

"My happiness is more than bountiful."

"I am valuable."

“ In am successful.”

"I am loved."

"I am happy & fulfilled."

"I radiate positivity."

"I am happy and satisfied."

Made in the USA
Columbia, SC
06 June 2025